CRACK IT

AN INTERVIEW BOOK FOR EVERY PHARMACEUTICAL FRESHER

PRACHI BARBHAIYA AND BHAVINI PATEL

ISBN 978-1-68554-507-9

"This book is dedicated to all the curious pharma freshers and readers – who are considering Pharmacy as their field of study, undergraduate students who are struggling to choose their major/ minor, and postgraduates who are looking to pursue their career in pharmacy."

Contents

About Author

Prachi Barbhaiya is the founder of Virgo Pharma, a leading healthcare writing service provider in the city. She has done Master in Quality Assurance from Gujarat Technological University. With writing skills in her hereditary, she has been awarded as COLUMNIST in 2014. She has vast experience in dealing with generic as well as ethical medicines, hospital surgical and medical writing. She has guided many pharmaceutical freshers and young aspirants with building CVs, thesis writing, research paper writing etc.

When she is not writing, Prachi spends most of her time reading, exploring the secrets of nature, travelling the world or catching her favourite web shows.

Keep in touch with Prachi via the web:

Gmail: virgopharma022@gmail.com

Facebook: www.facebook.com/virgopharma022

Instagram: www.instagram.com/virgopharma022

Bhavini Patel has done Master in Quality Assurance from Gujarat Technological University. She has vast experience in export, hospital surgical and regulatory affairs. Being regulatory affairs professional, she is an expert in documentation and presentation. With thorough knowledge of analytical skills, she has guided many pharmaceutical aspirants and her juniors for their project work.

Always with new thoughts which can be uplifting for the pharmacy profession, here she presents her first book to all the pharmaceutical freshers. She is a bookaholic and spends most of her time reading, doing creative experiments, meeting healthcare aspirants or goes on a self-driven long bike drive.

Keep in touch with Bhavini via the web:

Gmail: bhavinipatel151293@gmail.com

Facebook: www.facebook.com/bhavinipatel151293

I

PHARMACIST/ HOSPITAL PHARMACIST Q&A

Q. Define pharmacy.

A. Pharmacy is that clinical health science that links medical and life science with chemistry and it is charged with the invention, production, disposal, safe and effective use, and control of medicines and drugs.

Q. Define health.

A. Health, according to the World Health Organization, is "a state of complete physical, mental and social well-being and not merely the absence of disease and infirmity".

Q. Define generic drug.

A. Generic drug according to FDA is "a medication created to be the same as an existing approved brand-name drug in dosage form, safety, strength, route of administration, quality, and performance characteristics".

Q. What according to you is the most important business aspect of being a pharmacist?

A. Providing great patient care is probably the best thing you can do for the business side of pharmacy. Patients who feel they receive care and have a pharmacist who is knowledgeable and cares about them individually will continue to frequent that pharmacy.

Q. What is the responsibility of a pharmacist?

- Manage a drug store
- Advising patients and physicians
- Verifying the accuracy of prescription
- Reviewing possible side effects
- Assigning correct dosage
- Recommending the most appropriate non-prescription drug
- Give information to the patient about drug interaction

Q. What do you mean by Schedule H and Schedule X drug?

A. Schedule H- List of Prescribed drugs

Schedule X- Drugs whose import, manufacture and sale, labelling and packing are governed by special provision

Q. What is warfarin and what are some of the drugs it interacts with and should be avoided?

A. Warfarin is a drug used as an anti-coagulant, and it is used in a patient who is at high risk of heart attack due to a blood clots.

It should be avoided in combination with:

- Aspirin
- Clopidogrel
- Dipyridamole
- LMWHs (Low Molecular Weight Heparins)
- NSAIDs
- Ticlopidine
- Unfractionated heparin
- Vitamin K and its combinations

Q. Full form of NABP, NABH, NABL

- NABP: National Association of Boards of Pharmacy
- NABH: National Accreditation Board for Hospitals and Healthcare Providers
- NABL: National Accreditation Board for Testing and Calibration Laboratories

Q. What information should be there on a prescription for controlled drugs?

A. For a controlled drug prescription should cover all this information:

- Date of issue
- Patient name and address
- Practitioner name, address and DEA registration number
- Drug name
- Drug strength
- Dosage form
- Quantity prescribed
- Directions for use
- Number of refills authorized
- Manual signature of the prescriber

Q. How will you dispense narcotic drugs to the patient?

A. For narcotic drugs, prescription has to be preserved for two years. While dispensing narcotic drugs, mention the date of issue and quantity issued on the prescription with the signature of the pharmacist on it.

Q. How do you manage expiry?

A. Every month medicines are removed from the stock three months before the expiry and has to be kept in a separate rack and return to the respective distributor.

Q. Give some examples of life-saving drugs.

- Adrenaline
- Glucagon
- Glycerol trinitrate

Q. Color codes in hospital.

- Code RED: Fire
- Code BLUE: Cardiac Arrest
- Code ORANGE: Disaster
- Code YELLOW: Missing Patient
- Code BLACK: Bomb Threat

Q. Full form of ABC analysis, VED, FSN, SDE.

- ABC analysis- Activity Based Costing or Always Better Control analysis (70%, 20%, 10%)
- VED- Vital, Essential, Desirable
- FSN- Fast Moving, Slow Moving, Non-Moving
- SDE- Scarce, Difficult, Easily Available

Q. Give some examples of drugs to be kept in the refrigerator (cold chain management).

- All insulins
- Latanoprost eye drops
- Antibiotics
- All vaccines
- Interferons
- All Suppositories

Q. Give five brand names of Paracetamol tablets.

- Metacin
- Crocin
- Calpol
- Perfalgan
- Febrex

Q. Give five names of Amoxycillin and Clavulanic acid combination tablet.

- Augmentin
- Moxikind CV
- Clavam
- Moxclav
- Novamox CV

Q. Give some examples of anti-viral drugs.

- Acyclovir
- Entecavir
- Ganciclovir
- Lamivudine
- Oseltamivir
- Remdesivir
- Tenofovir
- Valaciclovir
- Zidovudine

Q. Give some examples of vaccines.

- Influvac (Influenza)
- Rabipur (Rabivax S vaccine)

- Pneumovax 23 (Pneumococcal vaccine)
- Tenivac (Tetanus)
- Tybar (typhoid vaccine)

Note: Some other questions which can be asked and whose answer vary from person to person:

- How do you read any prescription?
- What if prescribed brand is not available at your store?
- How do you manage short items?
- What would you do if you have any drug in stock and suddenly doctor stop prescribing that brand?

II
QUALITY CONTROL Q&A

Q. Define quality control.

A. Quality control is a system of maintaining standards in manufactured products by testing a sample of the output against the specification. It may include chemical, physical or microbiological testing of a pharmaceutical product.

Q. What is the difference between quality control and quality assurance.

Quality Control: Identification of defect, Reactive process, Product based approach, E.g., Inspection and testing

Quality Assurance: Prevention of defect, Proactive process, Process-based approach, E.g., Quality Audit

Q. Full form of GMP, cGMP, GLP.

- GMP: Good Manufacturing Process
- cGMP: Current Good Manufacturing Process
- GLP: Good Laboratory Practice

Q. Enlist few responsibilities which come under quality control.

- Sampling of raw and packing material
- Testing of raw material, packing material, in-process, finished product and stability batches
- Sampling and testing of water
- Calibration of instruments
- Preparation of specification of raw, packing, in-process and finished products
- Preparation of standard test procedure of raw, packing, in-process and finished products and reporting of the result after analysis and preparation of COA

Q. Define calibration.

A. A demonstration that a specific instrument or device produces results within specified limits by comparison with those produced by a traceable standard over an appropriate range of measurements.

Q. Give some HPLC calibration parameters.

- Flow rate accuracy measurement- Pump
- Linearity of the response check and wavelength accuracy check-Detector
- Carryover check and linearity- Autosampler
- Calibration of column oven and sample cooler

Q. Define deviation.

A. Any unwanted event that represents a departure from approved processes or procedures or instruction or specification or established standard or from what is required.

Q. Define chromatography.

A. Chromatography is an analytical technique commonly used for separating a mixture of chemical substances into their individual components so that the individual components can be thoroughly analysed.

Q. Full form of HPLC, LCMS, UPLC, TLC, GC.

- HPLC-High Performance Liquid Chromatography
- LCMS-Liquid chromatography-mass spectrometry
- UPLC-Ultra-High-Performance Liquid Chromatography
- TLC- Thin Layer Chromatography
- GC- Gas Chromatography

Q. Difference between Stationary Phase and Mobile Phase.

- Stationary Phase- Does not Move with the sample
- Mobile Phase- Moves with the sample

Q. Full form of OOT and OOS.

- OOT-Out of trend
- OOS-Out of specification

Q. Define stability.

A. Stability of a pharmaceutical product means how long it can maintain its original form for the duration of the shelf life assigned to it and should comply with the specification without any visible changes under the influence of various environmental factors like temperature and humidity and light.

Q. Define shelf life.

A. The period of time during which a drug product, if stored correctly, is expected to comply with the specifications determined by stability studies on a number of batches of the product.

It is used to establish the expiry date of each product.

Q. Full form of LOD and LOQ.

- LOD: Limit of detection
- LOQ: Limit of Quantification

Q. Range of Ultraviolet (UV) and visible spectroscopy.

- Ultraviolet Spectroscopy- 200-400 nm
- Visible Spectroscopy- 400-800 nm

Q. Define pH and its range.

A. pH is the negative logarithm of hydrogen ion concentration. Its range is from 0-14.

Q. Which detectors are used in HPLC?

A. UV detector, IR detector, Fluorescence detector, Mass spectroscopy, LC-MS

Some other questions which can be asked:

1. Which instruments you have handled in your college?

2. Which model of UV spectrometer, HPLC, fluidized bed dryer, IR, DSC have you handled?

III

QUALITY ASSURANCE Q&A

Q. Full form of ICH and its classification.

A. ICH- International Council for Harmonization of Technical Requirements for Pharmaceuticals for Human Use.

- Q: Quality Guidelines (E.g., Stability testing, impurity testing etc.) (Q1-Q10)
- S: Safety Guidelines (E.g., carcinogenicity, genotoxicity testing, Immunotoxicity etc.)
- E: Efficacy Guidelines (dose response studies, GCP, clinical safety)
- M: Multidisciplinary Guidelines (M1- MedDRA terminology, ESTRI, CTD)

ESTRI- Electronic Standards for Transmission of Regulatory Information

Q. Give overview for ICH guidelines.

A. **Quality**

- Q1A(R2) stability testing in new drugs and products (revised guideline)
- Q1B Photostability testing
- Q1C Stability testing: new dosage forms
- Q1D Bracketing and matrixing designs for stability testing of drug substances and drug products
- Q1E Evaluation of stability data
- Q1F Stability data package for registration in climatic zones iii and iv
- Q2A Definitions and terminology: analytical validation
- Q2B Methodology
- Q3A Impurity testing in new drug substances
- Q3B Impurities in dosage forms: addendum to the guideline on impurities in new drug substances
- Q3C Impurities: residual solvents
- Q3D Impurities: elemental impurities
- Q4 Pharmacopeial harmonization
- Q5A Viral safety evaluation
- Q5B Genetic stability
- Q5C Stability of biotechnology products
- Q5D Cell substrates
- Q5E Comparability of biotechnological/biological products subject to changes in their manufacturing process
- Q6A Specifications: test procedures, and acceptance criteria for new drug substances and products
- Q6B Specifications: Test procedure and acceptance criteria for biotechnological/biological
- Q7 GMP for active pharmaceutical ingredients
- Q8 Pharmaceutical development
- Q9 Quality risk management
- Q10 Pharmaceutical quality system
- Q11 Development and Manufacture of Drug Substances

- Q12 Life cycle management

Safety

- S1A Guideline on the need for carcinogenicity studies of pharmaceuticals
- S1B Testing for carcinogenicity of pharmaceuticals
- S1C(R2) Dose selection for carcinogenicity studies of pharmaceuticals
- S2(R1) Guidance on genotoxicity testing and data interpretation for pharmaceuticals intended for human use
- S3A Note for guidance on toxicokinetic: the assessment of systemic exposure in toxicity studies
- S3B Pharmacokinetics: guidance for repeated dose tissue distribution studies
- S4 Duration of chronic toxicity testing in animals (rodent and non-rodent toxicity testing)
- S5(R2) Detection of toxicity to reproduction for medicinal products and toxicity to male fertility
- S6 Preclinical safety evaluation of biotechnology-derived pharmaceuticals
- S7A Safety pharmacology studies for human pharmaceuticals
- S7B The non-clinical evaluation of the potential for delayed ventricular repolarization (qt interval prolongation) by human pharmaceuticals
- S8 Immunotoxicity studies for human pharmaceuticals
- S9 Non-clinical evaluation for anti-cancer pharmaceutical

Efficacy

- E1 The extent of population exposure to assess clinical safety
- E2A Clinical safety data management
- E2B(R2) Maintenance of the ICH guideline on clinical safety data management

- E2B(R3) Revision of the ICH guideline on clinical safety data management data elements for transmission of individual case safety reports
- E2C(R1) Clinical safety data management: periodic safety update reports for marketed drugs
- E2D Post-approval safety data management: definitions and standards for expedited reporting
- E2E Pharmacovigilance planning
- E2F Development safety update report
- E3 Structure and content of clinical study reports
- E4 Dose-response information to support drug registration
- E5(R1) Ethnic factors in the acceptability of foreign clinical data
- E6(R1) Guideline for Good Clinical Practice
- E7 Studies in support of special populations: geriatrics
- E8 General considerations for clinical trials
- E9 Statistical principles for clinical trials
- E10 Choice of control group and related issues in clinical trials
- E11 Clinical investigation of medicinal products in the pediatric population
- E12 Principles for clinical evaluation of new antihypertensive drugs
- E14 The clinical evaluation of qt/qtc interval prolongation and proarrhythmic potential for non-antiarrhythmic drugs

- E15 Definitions for genomic biomarkers, pharmacogenomics, pharmacogenetics, genomic data and sample coding categories
- E16 Genomic biomarkers related to drug response: context, structure and format of qualification submissions

Multi-disciplinary

- M1 MedDRA terminology
- M2 (R2) Electronic transmission of individual case safety reports message specification
- M3(R2) Guidance on non-clinical safety studies for the conduct of human clinical trials and marketing authorization for pharmaceuticals
- M4 Organization of the common technical document for the registration of pharmaceuticals for human use
- M4E(R1) The common technical document for the registration of pharmaceuticals for human use: efficacy
- M4Q(R1) The common technical document for the registration of pharmaceuticals for human use: quality
- M4S(R2) The common technical document for the registration of pharmaceuticals for human use: safety
- M5 Data elements and standards for drug dictionaries

Q. Give classification of climatic zone as per ICH.

- Zone I- Temperate zone
- Zone II- Mediterranean/ Sub tropical zone
- Zone III- Hot dry zone
- Zone IV a- Hot humid/tropical zone
- Zone IV b- Hot/very humidity

India falls under zone III/zone IV b climatic zone.

Q. Define SOP.

A. Standard Operating Procedure (SOP) is a certain type of document that describes in a step-by-step outline form how to perform a particular task or operation.

Q. Define qualification.

A. The action of proving that any equipment or process work correctly and consistently and produces the expected result. Qualification is part of, but not limited to a validation process.

Q. Full form of IQ, OQ, PQ.

- IQ-Installation Qualification
- OQ- Operational Qualification
- PQ- Performance Qualification

Q. Why do we consider three consecutive runs/batches for process validation? Why not two or four?

- First batch quality is accidental (co-incidental)
- Second batch quality is regular (accidental)
- Third batch quality is validation(conformation)

In 2 batch we cannot assure the reproducibility of data, 4 batches can be taken but the time and cost are involved.

Q. Define validation and give its type.

A. Validation is establishing documented evidence that provide high degree of assurance that specific process will consistently produce a product meet its predetermined specification and quality attributes.

There are mainly four types of validation:

- Prospective Validation

- Concurrent Validation
- Retrospective Validation
- Revalidation (Periodic and After Change)

Q. Define deviation.

A. Any unwanted event that represents a departure from approved processes or procedures or instruction or specification or established standard or from what is required.

Q. Define change control.

A. It is an approved procedure which is taken to change in any documents, standard operating procedures, specification, process parameters and change in batch size etc.

Change control is raised by user department as per requirement and finally the change control is approved by quality assurance.

Q. Define CAPA.

A. CAPA- Corrective Action- Preventive Action

Corrective Action-An action taken to eliminate the cause of the existing deviation, incident or problem in order to prevent its recurrence (occurring again).

Preventive action- An action taken to eliminate the cause of potential deviation, incident or problem in order to prevent its occurrence (an incident or event).

Q. What is IPQA? Give its check points.

A. IPQA- In Process-Quality Assurance

Check points can be enlisted as:

- Production IPQA
- Raw Material Store (RM) IPQA
- Manufacturing (Granulation / Oral Liquid/ Lubrication) IPQA

- Compression IPQA
- Capsule filling and polishing IPQA
- Packing process IPQA

Q. Give full form of MFR, BMR, BPR, BPCR.

- BMR- Batch Manufacturing Record
- MFR- Master Formula Record
- BPR- Batch Packing Record
- BPCR- Batch Production and Control Records

IV

PRODUCTION Q&A

Q. Define production.

A. All operations involved in the preparation of a pharmaceutical product, from receipt of raw materials through the completion of a finished product i.e., from raw material receipt to finished product dispatch is termed as production.

Q. Define Active Pharmaceutical Ingredient (API).

A. A substance or a bulk pharmaceutical chemical that is intended to furnish pharmacological activity or another direct effect in the diagnosis, cure, mitigation, treatment, or prevention of the disease or to affect the structure or any function of the body of man or other animals.

Q. Which are the different types of formulation available in the market?

- Tablet
- Capsule
- Ointment

- Cream
- Dusting powder
- Syrup
- Solution
- Suspension
- Emulsion
- Inhaler
- Aerosol
- Paste
- Gel
- Suppositories
- Patches
- Tincture
- Liniment
- Gargle
- Mouth wash
- Throat paint
- Eye drops
- Ear drops
- Nasal drops
- Enema
- Douches
- Lozenges

Q. Define tablet.

A. Tablets are the compressed solid dosage forms each containing a unit dose of one or more medicaments and intended for oral administration.

Q. What are the different types of tablets?

- Enteric-coated tablets
- Chewable tablets
- Orally disintegrating tablets

- Sublingual tablets
- Effervescent tablets

Q. Which types of formulation require a hardness test and what is its importance?

A. Hardness test or crushing strength test is performed on the tablet dosage form.

This measures the degree of force required to break a tablet. If the tablet is too hard it may not disintegrate in the required period of time and if it is too soft it will not withstand coating and packing.

It depends on several factors like the amount of lubricant used, space between upper and lower punch at the time of compression etc.

Q. Define the disintegration test and give its criteria.

A. It is the time required for the tablet/capsule to break into particles under a given set of conditions for a group of tablets/capsules.

The cycle of the shaft holding the tube basket limit is 29-32 cycles per minute and distance covered by the shaft basket is 50-60 mm and the beaker temperature is 35 to 39 ° C.

Q. Give disintegration time for tablet and capsule.

- Uncoated Tablet 15 min as per BP
- Uncoated Tablet 30 min as per USP
- Gastro-resistant capsule DT 2 hrs. without a disk in 0.1 M HCl and phosphate buffer pH 6.8 for a further 60 min as per BP
- Hard and Soft gelatin capsule DT 30 min as per BP and USP

Q. What is the dissolution test?

A. It measures the amount of drug released from the dosage form. It is important for bioavailability and therapeutic effect.

Q. What is the pH of the dissolution medium?

A. 1.2 to 6.8

Q. Define friability test, calculation and its limit.

A. Friability is defined as the percentage of weight loss of powder from the surface of the tablets due to mechanical action and the test is performed to measure the weight loss during transportation.

Friability (%) =W1– W2/W1X100 Where,

W1 = Weight of Tablets (Initial / Before tumbling) and

W2 = Weight of Tablets (After Tumbling or friability)

Limit: Friability (%) = Not More Than 1.0 %

- Number of rotations: 100rpm
- Fall height of the tablets: 6 inches
- Minimum 20 tablets are taken

Q. What are the in-processes checks parameters during tablet compression?

A. Appearance, Group weight, Individual weight variation, Uniformity of weight, Thickness, Diameter, Hardness, friability, speed of the machine, compaction force, die fill depth and Disintegration time.

Q. What are the in-processes checks parameters during capsule filling?

A. Appearance, Group weight of filled capsule, Individual weight of filled capsule, Net fill content of the powder, locking length and Disintegration time.

Q. What are the in-processes checks parameters during tablet coating?

A. Appearance, Inlet temperature, outlet temperature, pan RPM, Gun distance from tablet bed, spray rate, weight gain, group weight of coated tablets, individual weight of coated tablets, and thickness.

Q. Why the microbial test is required for capsules?

A. As the capsule is made up of gelatin, it is necessary to ensure the lack of growth of bacteria and mould. Hence microbial test has to be performed.

Q. Give some names of tablet and capsule machine.

- Rotosort
- Rotofill
- Rotoweigh
- Wurster

Q. What are the types of tablet processing problems?

- Mottling– unequal colour distribution of a tablet
- Capping– Partial or complete separation of a tablet top or bottom crowns
- Lamination– Separation of tablets into two or more layers
- Picking– Because of adhesion to the punch faces, localized portion missing on the surface of the tablet
- Sticking– Adhesion of tablet localized portion to the punch faces resulting in a rough and dull appearance

Q. Define excipient.

A. Excipients are the non-drug component (additives) used to convert pharmacologically active compounds in a pharmaceutical dosage form suitable for the administration of patients.

Examples: Magnesium stearate, purified talc, starch etc.

Q. Categorize excipients.

A. Diluents, binders and adhesive, fillers, disintegrants, lubrications, glidants, flow promoters, colours, flavours and sweetness.

Q. Give examples of diluents.

- Microcrystalline cellulose (MCC) (Avicel 101 powder form, Avicel 102 granular form)
- Lactose
- Sucrose
- Starch
- Mannitol
- Sodium carbonate

Q. Give examples of disintegrants.

- Cross carmelose sodium
- Crosspovidone
- Sodium starch glidant

Q. Give examples of binders.

- Polyvinyl pyrollidine
- Starch paste
- HPMC
- CMC
- Acacia
- Tragacanth
- Alginates etc.

Q. Give examples of glidants.

- Aerosil

- Talc
- Silica etc.

Q. Give examples of lubricants used in tablets.

- Magnesium stearate
- Calcium stearate
- Zinc stearate
- Stearic acid
- Myistic acid
- Palmitic acid etc

Q. What is the difference between ampoule and vial?
A. Ampoule- Single dose unit
Vial- Multiple dose unit
Q. Define emulsion.
A. An emulsion is a biphasic liquid preparation containing two immiscible liquids, one of which is dispersed as minute globules into the other. The liquid which is converted into minute globules is named the "dispersed phase" and the liquid in which the globules are dispersed is called the "continues phase "
Q. Give examples of emulsifying agents.
A. Albumin, glycerol, propylene glycol, soaps etc.
Q. Define suspension and give examples.
A. Suspensions are the biphasic liquid dosage form in which solid substances are suspended in a liquid medium and are stabilized by the addition of suspending agent.
Examples: Gum Acacia, Tragacanth, Agar, gelatin, carboxymethyl cellulose, milk of magnesia etc.
Q. What are the different types of capsules?

- Hard gelatin capsule

- Soft gelatin capsule

Q. What is the biggest and smallest capsule size?

A. The biggest capsule size -000 and smallest capsule size – 5.

Q. How do you evaluate the flow property of powder?

A. Flow property of powder can be evaluated by measuring

- Carr's index
- Hausner ratio
- Angle of repose

Q. What is the expiry date of the empty shell capsule and how it is preserved?

A. Expiry: 2 to 5 years

Preservation: Hard gelatin capsules have a water content of 12%-15%. When moisture levels are below 12%, capsule brittleness becomes a problem. When moisture levels are above this range, deformation becomes apparent.

To maintain capsule integrity, empty capsules should be stored in closed containers under controlled conditions of 15°-25°C and 35%-55% RH.

Q. What is the difference between antiseptic and disinfectant?

A. Antiseptic-An agent that inhibits or destroys microorganisms on living tissue including skin, oral cavities, and open wounds

Disinfectant-A chemical or physical agent that destroys or removes vegetative forms of harmful microorganisms when applied to a surface

Q. What is IPQA test for parenteral?

A. Clarity test (visual method, coulter counter method, light obscuration technique), leakage testing (visual method, bubble test, dye test), fill volume test, pH, pyrogen testing (Rabbit fever, LAL test), assay for drug content, membrane filtration test, water attack test, powder glass test.

Q. Give full form of LAL test.

A. Limulus amoebocyte lysate test

Q. When performing the 'uniformity of weight' of the dosage unit, how many tablets/capsules can deviate from the established limit?

A. Not more than two of the individual weights can deviate from the average weight by more than the percentage given in the pharmacopoeia, and none can deviate more than twice that percentage.

V
CLINICAL RESEARCH ORGANIZATION Q&A

Q. Define clinical trial.

A. Clinical research means any kind of investigation in human subjects which aims to discover/check the clinical, pharmacological, and other pharmacodynamic effects of an investigational product that follow a pre-defined protocol.

Q. Define informed consent.

A. Informed consent is the process of learning the key facts about a clinical trial before deciding whether or not to participate. However, it is important to note that informed consent is not a contract and the participant can withdraw from the trial at any time.

Q. Who sponsors clinical trials?

A. Clinical trials are sponsored or funded by different organizations or individuals such as physicians, medical institutions, foundations, voluntary groups and pharmaceutical companies. Also, some of the federal agencies such as the National Institutes of Health (NIH), the Department of Defense (DOD), and the Department of Veteran's Affairs (VA) sponsor clinical trials.

Q. Define protocol.

A. A protocol is a study plan of clinical trials. A protocol describes what types of people may participate in the trial; the schedule of tests, procedures, medications, and dosages; and the length of the study.

Q. Define placebo.

A. A placebo is an inactive pill, liquid, or powder that has no treatment value.

In clinical trials, experimental treatments are often compared with placebos to assess the experimental treatment's effectiveness. In some kind of trial, the participants in the control group will receive a placebo instead of an active drug or experimental treatment which is supposed to be given.

Q. What do you know about the drug development process?

A. Drug development is the entire process of bringing a new pharmaceutical drug to the market. It involves following steps:

Step 1: Discovery and Development

Step 2: Preclinical Research

Step 3: Clinical Research

Step 4: FDA Drug Review

Step 5: FDA Post-Market Drug Safety Monitoring

Q. Describe phases of clinical trials.

A. These are the following phases of the clinical trials:

- Preclinical: Testing of drug in non-human subjects to gather efficacy, toxicity and pharmacokinetic information (in vitro and in vivo only)
- Phase 0: Pharmacokinetics; particularly oral bioavailability and half-life of the drug in approx. 10 people
- Phase 1: Test a new drug or treatment to a small group of people (20-80) to evaluate its safety
- Phase 2: The experimental drug or treatment is given to a large group of people (100-300) to see drug efficacy and side effects
- Phase 3: The experimental drug or treatment is given to a large group of people (1000-3000) to see its effectiveness, monitor side effects and compare it to commonly used treatments
- Phase 4: The 4-phase study includes the post marketing studies including the drug's risk, benefits etc.

Q. Explain types of clinical trials.

- Single Blind Study- When the patients are not aware of which treatment they receive
- Double Blind Study- When the patients and the investigator are unaware of the treatment group assigned
- Triple Blind Study- Triple blind study is when patients, investigator, and the project team are unaware of the treatments administered

Q. Define Clinical Study Report (CSR).
A. A clinical study report (CSR) on a clinical trial is a document, typically very long, providing much detail about the methods and results of a trial.

Q. What does ICD code mean?

A. International Classification of Diseases, Tenth Revision (ICD-10).

Q. Why SAP is important?

A. SAP is the document that contains detailed information regarding the statistical methods and study objectives to help in the production of the Clinical Study Report (CSR) including figures, summary tables, and subject data listings for protocol.

VI
REGULATORY AFFAIRS Q&A

Q. Define Regulatory Affairs.

A. Regulatory Affairs act as the interface between the pharmaceutical industry and drug regulatory authorities across the world. It is mainly involved in the registration of new or abbreviated drug products in respective countries prior to their marketing.

Q. What are the goals of RA Professionals?

- Protection of human health
- Ensuring safety, efficacy and quality of drugs
- Ensuring appropriateness and accuracy of product information

Q. What are the roles of RA Professionals?

- Act as a liaison with regulatory agencies
- Preparation of organized and scientifically valid NDA, ANDA, INDA, MAA, DMF submissions

- Ensure adherence and compliance with all the applicable cGMP, ICH, GCP, CLP guidelines, regulations and laws
- Providing expertise and regulatory intelligence in translating regulatory requirements into practical workable plans
- Advising the companies on regulatory aspects and climate that would affect their proposed activities

Q. What is a dossier in regulatory affairs?

A. Regulatory Dossier means all regulatory documents and filings registered with a Drug Regulatory Authority for a Marketing Authorization containing the administrative, safety, efficacy, quality, non-clinical and clinical data and CMC data for the Drug Product as it may change from time to time.

Q. What does a regulatory framework mean?

A. Regulatory Framework means any laws, regulations, decrees and policies officially developed and approved by the government, for the purposes of regulating the solid waste generation, collection, transport, recycling, reuse, treatment and disposal.

Q. What is an Investigational New Drug (IND) application?

A. It is an application which is filed with FDA to get approval for legally testing and experimental drug on human subjects in the USA.

Q. What is a New Drug Application (NDA)?

A. It is an application which is filed with FDA to market a new pharmaceutical for sale in USA.

Q. What is an Abbreviated New Drug Application (ANDA)?

A. It is an application filed with FDA, for a U.S. generic drug approval for an existing medication or approved drug.

Q. What are the Chemical Classification Codes for NDA?

1: New molecular entity (NME)

2: New ester, new salt, or other noncovalent derivatives

3: New formulation

4: New combination

5: New Manufacturer

6: New indication

7: Drug already marketed but without an approved NDA

8: OTC switch

Q. What is a Generic Drug Product?

A. A generic drug product is the one that is comparable to an innovator drug product in dosage form, strength, route of administration, quality, performance characteristics and intended use.

Q. What is DMF?

A. A Drug Master File is a submission to the Food and Drug Administration (FDA) that is used to provide confidential detailed information about facilities, processes or articles used in the manufacturing, processing, packaging, and storing of drugs.

Q. Important Facts regarding DMF's.

- It is submitted to FDA to provide confidential information
- Its submission is not required by law or regulations
- It is neither approved nor disapproved
- It is filed with FDA to support NDA, IND, ANDA another DMF or amendments and supplements to any of these
- It is not required when the applicant references their own information

Q. What are the types of DMF's?

A. Type 1: Manufacturing Site, Facilities, Operating Procedures and personnel (No longer accepted by FDA)

Type 2: Drug Substance, Drug Substance Intermediate and Material used in their Preparation or Drug Product

Type 3: Packaging Material

Type 4: Excipient, Colorant, Flavor, Essence or Material Used in their Preparation

Type 5: FDA Accepted Reference Information

Q. What is Marketing Authorization Application?

A. It is an application filed with the relevant authority in Europe to market a drug or medicine.

As per UK's MHRA:

Application for new active substances is described as 'full applications.

Applications for medicines containing existing active substances are described as 'abbreviated' or 'abridged applications.

Q. What is an ASMF?

A. Active substance master file is a submission which is made to EMA, MHRA or any other Drug Regulatory Authority in Europe to provide confidential intellectual property of 'know-how' of the manufacturer of the active substance.

Q. What are the types of Active substances for which ASMFs are submitted?

- New active substances
- Existing active substances not included in the European Pharmacopoeia or the pharmacopoeia of an EU Member State
- Pharmacopeial active substances included in the Ph. Eur. Or in the pharmacopoeia of an EU Member State

Q. What is the difference between DMF and ASMF (with respect to submission)?

A. ASMF is submitted as Applicant's Part (Open part) and Restricted Part (Closed Part) There is no differentiation of DMF's into parts.

Q. What is ICH?

A. International Conference on Harmonization of Technical Requirements for Registration of Pharmaceutical for Human Use (ICH): is a project that brings together the regulatory authorities of Europe, Japan and the United States and experts from the pharmaceutical industry in the three regions to discuss scientific and technical aspects of pharmaceutical product registration.

Q. What is CTD?

A. The Common Technical Document (CTD) is a set of specifications for the application dossier, for the registration of medicines and is designed to be used across Europe, Japan and US. Information like Quality, Safety and Efficacy is assembled in a common format through CTD.

Q. What are the ICH guidelines to be referred for preparation of registration dossier/ application of medicines (With respect to format and contents in each module)?

- M4 Guidelines
- M4Q Guidelines
- M4S Guidelines
- M4E Guidelines

Q. What are the modules in CTD?

A. CTD is divided in 5 modules:

- Module 1: Administrative information and prescribing information
- Module 2: Common Technical Document Summaries
- Module 3: Quality
- Module 4: Nonclinical Study Reports (toxicology studies)
- Module 5: Clinical Study Reports (clinical studies)

Q. What is the difference between CTD and ACTD?

A. The ACTD consists of Parts I to IV which have subsections A to F whereas ICH-CTD has 5 Modules with subsections that are numbered. The administrative data of Part I is part of ACTD whereas Module 1 of ICH-CTD is purely country-specific.

Q. Give Drug Regulatory Agencies full names

- CDSCO – Central Drugs Standard Control Organization (India)
- USFDA – United States Food and Drug Administration (United States of America)
- MHRA – Medicines and Healthcare products Regulatory Agency (United Kingdom)
- EMA – European Medicines Agency (European Union)
- TGA – Therapeutic Goods Administration (Australia)

Q. What are the procedures for approval of drugs in EU?

- Centralized Procedure (CP)
- Decentralized Procedure (DCP)
- Mutual Recognition Procedure (MRP)
- National Procedure (NP)

Q. What is Orange Book?

A. It is a commonly used name for the book "Approved Drug Products with Therapeutic Equivalence Evaluations" Which is published by USFDA. Which contains a list of drug products, approved on the basis of safety and effectiveness by the FDA under the Federal Food, Drug and Cosmetic Act.

Q. What is the full form of CEP?

A. Certificate of suitability of Monograph of European Pharmacopoeia

Q. What is CEP?

A. It is the certificate which is issued by Certification of Substances Division of European Directorate for the Quality of medicines (EDQM) when the manufacturer of a substance provides proof that the quality of the substance is suitably controlled by the relevant monographs of the European Pharmacopoeia.

Q. What is Pharma ROW Market?

A. United State (US) and the EU are the biggest and the most potential markets for in the world and are categorized under the regulated markets, whereas ROW (Rest of the World) market includes all the emerging markets like Brazil (LATAM), Tanzania (Africa), Russia (CIS), Hong Kong (ASIA), etc.

Q. Which products need FDA approval?

- Human and animal drug
- Medical biologics
- Medical devices
- Food (including animal food)
- Tobacco products
- Cosmetics
- Electronic products that emit radiation

VII
RESEARCH AND DEVELOPMENT Q&A

Q. Explain the term Aliquot and Diluent?

A. Aliquot: It is a measured sub-volume of the original sample and Diluent is the material with which the sample is diluted.

Q. What is molality?

A. Molality is the number of solutes that are present in 1 kg of a solvent.

Q. What is titration?

A. Titration is a process to determine the molarity of a base or an acid. In this process, a reaction is carried out between the known volumes of a solution with a known concentration, against the known volume of a solution with an unknown concentration.

Q. What is a buffer?

A. A buffer is an aqueous solution that has a highly stable pH. It is a mixture of a weak acid and its conjugate base or vice versa. Adding a small amount of base or acid to the buffer does not bring a major change in pH.

Q. What is a mole?

A. Mole is the unit used to define the number of chemical substances present in a substance.

Q. What is the difference between fractionation and distillation?

A. Both methods are used to separate the components present in the solution based on the melting points.

- Distillation: This technique is used when the boiling point of chemicals are different in the mixtures
- Fractionation: This technique is used when the boiling point of chemicals are close to each other in the mixtures

Q. Mention the formula to calculate the pH of a solution?

A. In order to calculate the pH of a solution use the formula pH= -log [H+] or pH = -log [H3O+].

Q. Define normality and molarity.

- Normality: Normality (N) is defined as the number of equivalents per litre of solution
- Molarity (M) is defined as the number of moles of solute per litre of solution

Q. Define oxidation and reduction reaction.

- Oxidation: When there is a loss of hydrogen or electrons OR gain of oxygen is known as an Oxidation reaction

- Reduction: When there is a gain of hydrogen or electron OR loss of oxygen is known as a reduction reaction

Q. In gas chromatography what is used as carrier gas and make-up gas?

A. In gas chromatography, nitrogen gas is used as carrier gas and makeup gas.

Q. Why Karl Fisher Factor Is 5?

A. 5 mg of water consuming 1 ml of KF reagent.

Q. Define accuracy and precision.

- Accuracy: It is the closeness of test results obtained by that method to the true value
- Precision: It is the degree of agreement among individual test results when the method is applied repeatedly to multiple sampling of a homogeneous sample

Q. Explain different types of precision.

- Repeatability: expresses the precision under the same operating conditions over a short interval of time. Repeatability is also termed intra-assay precision.
- Intermediate precision: expresses within-laboratories variations: different days, different analysts, different equipment, etc. It is also known as ruggedness
- Reproducibility: expresses the precision between laboratories (collaborative studies, usually applied to standardization of methodology

Q. Why six unit is used for precision?

A. Since it is performed as per ICH guidelines for validation. (Q2_R1).

Q. Define specificity.

A. Specificity is the ability to assess unequivocally the analyte in the presence of components which may be expected to be present such as impurities, degradants, matrix, etc.

Q. Define detection limit.

A. The detection limit of an individual analytical procedure is the lowest amount of analyte in a sample which can be detected but not necessarily quantitated under stated experimental conditions.

Q. Define quantitation limit.

A. The detection limit of an individual analytical procedure is the lowest amount of analyte in a sample that can be determined with acceptable accuracy and precision under the stated experimental conditions.

Q. Define linearity.

A. The linearity of an analytical procedure is its ability (within a given range) to obtain test results which are directly proportional to the concentration (amount) of analyte in the sample.

Q. Define range.

A. The range of an analytical procedure is the interval between the upper and lower concentration (amounts) of analyte in the sample (including these concentrations) for which it has been demonstrated that the analytical procedure has a suitable level of precision, accuracy and linearity.

Q. Define robustness.

A. The robustness of an analytical procedure is a measure of its capacity to remain unaffected by small, but deliberate variations in method parameters and provides an indication of its reliability during normal usage.

VIII
PHARMACO-VIGILANCE Q&A

Q. What is pharmacovigilance?

A. Pharmacovigilance is the science of collecting, monitoring, researching, assessing and evaluating information from healthcare providers and patients on the adverse effects of medications, biological products, herbalism and traditional medicines.

Q. What are the objectives in Pharmacovigilance?

A. Understanding the concepts of ADR, medical errors, public health significance, regulatory interventions, ADR monitoring schemes.

Q. What is the minimum criterion which is required for a valid case?

- An identifiable reporter
- An identifiable patient
- A suspect product
- An adverse drug events

Q. What is an Adverse Drug Event (ADE)?

A. Any untoward medical occurrence in a patient or clinical investigation subject when administered a pharmaceutical product. It does not necessarily have a causal relationship with the treatment.

Q. What is an Adverse Drug Reaction (ADR)?

A. An adverse drug reaction is a response to a drug which is noxious and unintended and which occurs at doses normally used in man for prophylaxis, diagnosis, or therapy of disease or for the modification of physiologic function.

Q. When do you consider an event to be serious?

A. If an event is associated with any one of the following, it is considered to be serious:

- Death
- Life threatening
- Hospitalization or prolongation of hospitalization.
- Congenital anomaly
- Disability
- Medically significant

Q. Name the regulatory bodies in USA, UK, Japan and India?

- USA: United States Food and drug administration (USFDA).
- UK: European Medicines Agency (EMEA).
- Japan: Ministry of Health, Labor and Welfare (MHLW).
- India: Central Drugs Standard Control Organization (CDSCO)

Q. What is Volume 9A?

A. Volume 9A brings together general guidance on the requirements, procedures, roles and activities in the field of pharmacovigilance, for both Marketing Authorization Holders (MAH) and Competent Authorities of medicinal products for human use.

Volume 9A is presented in four parts:

- Part I deals with Guidelines for Marketing Authorization Holders
- Part II deals with Guidelines for Competent Authorities and the Agency
- Part III provides the Guidelines for the electronic exchange of pharmacovigilance in the EU
- Part IV provides Guidelines on pharmacovigilance communication.

Q. When do you consider a case to be medically confirmed?

A. A case is considered to be medically confirmed if it contains at least one event confirmed or reported by an HCP (Health Care Professional).

Q. What do you mean by causality?

A. In Pharmacovigilance, causality is the relationship between the suspect product and the adverse drug event.

Q. Name some data elements in ICSR?

- Patient demographics: Age, gender and race.
- Suspect product details: Drug, dose, dosage form, therapy dates, therapy duration and indication.
- Adverse event details: Event, event onset date, seriousness criterion, event end date and latency.

Q. What do you mean by MedDRA?

A. Medical Dictionary for Regulatory Activities.

Q. Explain the hierarchy in MedDRA.

- System Organ Class (SOC)
- High Level Group Term (HLGT)
- High Level Term (HLT)
- Preferred Term (PT)
- Lower-Level Term (LLT)

Q. Give abbreviations of the below terms.

- SAE: Serious Adverse Event
- CIOMS: Council for International Organizations of Medical Sciences
- ADE: Adverse Drug Event
- SSAR: Suspected Serious Adverse Reaction
- ADR: Adverse Drug Reaction
- ICSR: Individual Case Safety Report
- PSUR: Periodic Safety Update Report
- ICH: The International Conference on Harmonization of Technical Requirements for Registration of Pharmaceuticals for Human Use
- HIPAA: Health Insurance Portability and Accountability Act
- ESTRI: Electronic Standards for the Transfer of Regulatory Information
- IBD: International Birth Date

Q. What do you know about E2a, E2b and E2c guidelines?

- E2a: E2a guidelines give standard definitions and terminology for key aspects of clinical safety reporting.

It also gives guidance on mechanisms for handling expedited (rapid) reporting of adverse drug reactions in the investigational phase of drug development

- E2b: E2b guidelines for the maintenance of clinical safety data management and information about the data elements for transmission of Individual Case Safety Reports
- E2c: E2c guidelines for the maintenance of clinical safety data management and information about the Periodic Safety Update Reports for marketed drugs

Q. What are the due dates for safety reporting?

A. Safety reporting due dates are 7 days for IND and 15 days for NDA reporting.

Q. What is PubMed?

A. PubMed is a free search engine accessing primarily the MEDLINE database of references and abstracts on life sciences and biomedical topics.

Q. What is GPP?

A. Good Pharmacovigilance Practice.

IX
MEDICAL WRITER Q&A

Q. What are referencing and citation in medical writing?

A. Citation is the specific source that is mentioned in the body of the paper, if a source is quoted directly the exact page number is to be included in a citation or it is incomplete. However, reference is a list of sources that are cited, the reference is written at the end of the paper.

Q. What is proof-reading?

A. A large part of many writing and editing roles involves the ability to proofread and edit the text to a high standard. It is the ability to identify and resolve mistakes such as grammatical, spelling or formatting errors.

Q. Role of medical writer in pharma industry.

A. A medical writer produce a structured document that depicts information in a clear and concise manner in relation to pharma and research organization. They can be regulatory medical writers or educational medical writers.

Q. Name any language editing software

A. Grammarly.

Q. What do you mean by referencing style?

A. A referencing style is a set of rules telling you how to acknowledge the thoughts, ideas and work of others in a particular way.

Q. What is the approach to citation? What tools are you familiar with?

A. I mostly use Mendeley since I can sign in on my desktop or use the website directly from any computer and sign into my account where I have a saved library of journal articles that can be added to a reference page in several different citation styles (i.e., AMA, MLA, or APA).

Q. What is LBL and what is its purpose?

A. Pharma LBL or Leave Behind Literature are pamphlets that Medical Representatives leave at doctor's or pharmacists' desks, so that they can be referred any time. They act as good reminders to doctors and healthcare professionals about the product key features and qualities.

Note: See Pharmacovigilance and clinical research Q&A as well. Pharmacovigilance, clinical research and medical writer Q&A are subject to ask in inter-coordination.

X

MEDICAL REPRESENTATIVE (MR) Q&A

Q. What is the role of a Medical Representative (MR)?

A. The pharma company's product are sold by the medical representatives, may it be medicine or a medical device. They create a valuable relationship with the customers. Their ultimate motto is to enhance the drug brand awareness in the market and acts as a mediator between the customer and the company.

Q. What are the challenges in being a pharmaceutical salesperson?

A. The true challenge for a pharma salesperson is to convince a doctor to switch from a drug or a particular brand that he or she is prescribing to their patients.

Q. What are the key responsibilities of a medical representative?

- Increase sales
- Increase awareness of a brand
- Increase market share
- Meet and exceed targets
- 6-7 calls per day and fixing appointments
- Manage the territory like a small business
- Build a relationship and convey product information

Q. How can you become a successful pharmaceutical representative?

A. Pharma sales is a high turnover business and to get into its foot requires:

- Positive approach
- Good network and focusing on a sales call
- Good communication skills
- Good product knowledge
- Understanding the market value of your product
- Good research on competitors and their sales target

Q. Explain why pharma sales are different from other sales?

A. Pharma sales is an indirect sales role. Pharma sales have no order to close or contract to sign.

Q. How you can convince a physician to switch to your drug?

A. To switch on to your prescribed drug, your first step is to

- Make your presence by setting small sales initially, let say, targeting 1 or 2 patient and target bigger later on
- Gain complete knowledge about the drug and observe the prescribing behaviour of the physician

- Use your product knowledge and other tools to make physicians understand your product
- Once the physician shows his confidence in the product, push him to prescribe your product for more patient

Q. Do you know any of our company products?

A. Before attending the interview visit their company website first. It gives you an idea about the company products along with which disease drugs they are selling/ interested in.

Q. How will you move forward after a series of rejections?

A. Every NO we hear in sales moves us one step closer to the next deal we will close. Sales is a game of numbers, and unless we are totally terrible in selling, or we sell a product which is a complete crap, we will eventually close some deals. We cannot avoid rejections in sales. But attitude towards rejection can be improved.

Q. What is Sales?

A. Sales are activities related to selling or the number of goods sold in a given targeted time period.

Q. Define pharma sales.

A. Sales of pharmaceutical products, which may include medicines, or surgical devices, consumables of any form, machines, and equipment used in surgeries is called pharma sales.

Q. What is pharma marketing? what are the ways through which pharma marketing is done?

A. Pharma Marketing or Pharmaceutical Marketing deals with advertising and promoting the pharmaceutical drugs with an intention to increase sales. It is also known as medico-marketing.

Common ways of pharma marketing are:

- Providing free samples.
- Pharmaceutical representatives promoting drugs directly to the doctors.
- Direct advertising of the drug to the user.
- Detailing to hospitals.
- Journal Ads.

Q. What is the Difference between Sales and Marketing?

A. The difference between sales and marketing is that sales focus on working directly with prospects to get them to convert, while marketing focuses on sparking interest in your products. Essentially, marketing is the first step to getting leads interested, while sales take that interest and nurture it.

Q. What do you mean by planning or market planning?

A. Market planning is the process of organizing and defining the marketing aims of a company and gathering strategies and tactics to achieve them.

Q. What do you mean by marketing strategy?

A. Marketing strategy is a process that allow an organization to concentrate its limited resources on the greatest opportunities to increase sales and achieve a sustainable competitive advantage.

Q. You are given a list of physicians from a particular area, how will you start?

A. Planning is very important before you start your work. Try to understand the area and prepare a strategy. Moreover, try to understand your customers and their sales potential.

Q. Is there any software available in the market to help to track their sales and progress?

A. Pharmaceutical specific ERP software are available in the market which can be useful to track the total number of sales, exact customer location; profit made quarterly, sales management, stock information from stockiest and so on.

Q. How would you reach a physician who does not see a representative?

- Try to communicate with their staff (receptionists, medical secretaries, practice nurses, etc.)
- Send him product information and literature through e-mail
- Drop literature regarding product to their clinics
- Invite him to speaker meetings and see him at CME meetings

Note: You are also supposed to ask some of the questions from anatomy.

E.g., Explain nervous system/digestive system/ respiratory system or on any topic the company have their maximum products.

XI
ACADEMICS/ PROFESSOR Q&A

Q. Tell us about yourself?

A. Talk about yourself, study, projects, core values you possess like professor.

Q. Tell us about your Dissertation?

A. Brief your project about. How it was unique and how you accomplished it.

Q. What is it about our department that interests you?

A. Talk about your favourite subject. Your knowledge in that subject and how can you co-relate with the department you have applied for.

Q. What can you offer us that someone else can't?

A. Student's attachment and communication is the main thing here. You being good at convincing power and friendly nature can be right candidate for the post.

Q. What teaching techniques do you use in classroom?

A. Any technique which can turn fruitful for student will be used. Mostly techniques like group discussion, flipped classroom (where student prepare the lesson before the class), self-learning, gamification or using any online tools are the techniques widely used.

Q. What funding sources are you aware of that might support your future research?

A. UGC, CSIR, DST, AICTE, AYUSH, DBT, ICMR, GUJCOST

Q. Can you tell me about research process?

A. It generally includes following steps:

- Identification of research problem
- Broad literature survey
- Hypothesis formulation
- Preparation of research design
- Determining sample design
- Data collection
- Analysis of data
- Hypothesis testing
- Generalizations and interpretation
- Preparation of the report or presentation of the result

Q. What can be the source for literature?

- Books and Journals
- Electronic Databases
- Bibliographic Databases
- Abstract Databases
- Full-Text Databases
- Govt. and Industry Reports
- Internet
- Research Dissertations / Thesis

Message To Readers:

Dear readers, we hope you will appreciate this small gesture of helping you out in building your career. We have given our best effort that every candidate from any department can read any kind of interview questions under one roof. Here we have included academic interview questions. However, below are the other introductory questions that are most commonly asked during the interview:

- Tell me something about yourself.
- Tell me about your strengths and weakness.
- Why should I hire you?
- Where do you see yourself five years from now?
- Are you willing to relocate or travel?
- What are your goals?
- THE SALARY QUESTION

Some of the major References/Resources we have used:

- LinkedIn
- Pharmatutor
- Pharmaguideline
- FDA, ICH and CDSCO website
- Scribd
- Pharmaclub
- Ambition Box

You can write us your honest feedback via mail on pbarbhaiya.94@gmail.com OR bhavinipatel151293@gmail.com

www.ingramcontent.com/pod-product-compliance
Lightning Source LLC
Chambersburg PA
CBHW050658250726
48662CB00002B/753